STRESS AND COPING MECHANISMS

Manage your stress and live a happier life

Written by Benjamin Fléron
Translated by Jessica Foster

PROPEL
YOUR BUSINESS FORWARD!

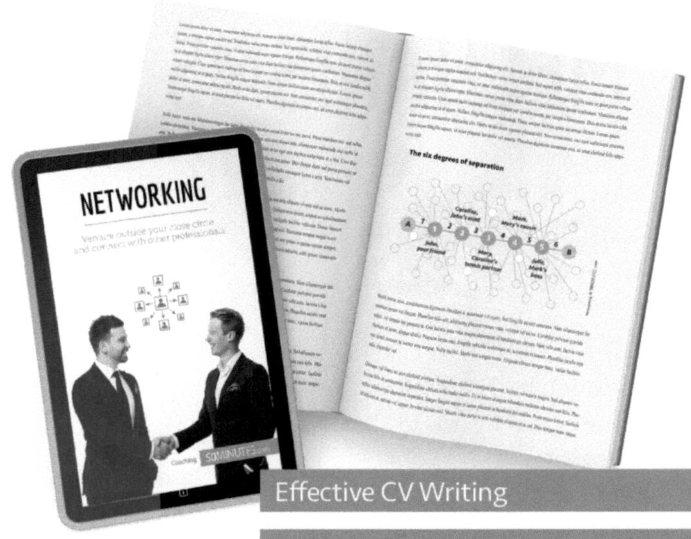

www.50minutes.com

STRESS AND COPING MECHANISMS — 1

COPING MECHANISMS: THE BASICS — 3

What is stress?
Stressful situations: a matter of framing
Coping strategies
Effectiveness and limitations of theory
Stress: an ally

TOP TIPS — 16

FAQS — 18

Where do I start in implementing a personal coping strategy?
What is the best way of overcoming stress?
How do I figure out the best coping style for me?
What harmful habits should I avoid?
Is it possible to live a stress-free life thanks to coping mechanisms?

OVER TO YOU — 22

FURTHER READING — 26

STRESS AND COPING MECHANISMS

- **Issue:** how can coping mechanisms help me to beat stress at work?
- **Uses:** coping offers an innovative approach to stress which allows us to identify different kinds of effective responses against anxiety and therefore to regain control and be able to work more efficiently.
- **Professional context:** work psychology, human resources, team management.
- **FAQs:**
  - Where do I start in implementing a personal coping strategy?
  - What is the best way of overcoming stress?
  - How do I figure out the best coping style for me?
  - What harmful habits should I avoid?
  - Is it possible to live a stress-free life thanks to coping mechanisms?

It is no secret that there are many sources of stress at work. Employers or employees, executives or labourers, freelancers or permanent staff, everyone has their own set of worries: budget cuts, restructuring, fierce competition, but also presentations to manage, strict deadlines to meet, complex files to deal with, etc. There are hundreds of sources of anxiety that can harm your productivity. So what if coping mechanisms could help you to deal with them?

We owe the conception of coping mechanisms to the American psychologist Richard S. Lazarus (1922-2002).

'Coping' refers to the mechanisms and strategies we use to deal with stressful situations and control – or at least reduce – the effects they have on us.

According to this theory, we are not powerless in the face of the stressful events we are regularly faced with, but rather we react to deal with them and thus try to regain control of the situation by responding to them in our own way. Think about the deep breaths you take before speaking in public, the habit you have of playing down a situation by repeating to yourself constantly that it will only take a minute when you have to relate some bad news to your boss, or the packets of sweets or cigarettes that are empty within five minutes when a stressful deadline is approaching. These are just some of the most common coping strategies.

But have you perhaps wondered if your coping mechanisms are really efficient? Are you sure you manage stressful situations that arise in the best way possible? Do you take advantage of them to improve your productivity rather than letting them slow you down? Research carried out on coping can help you to see it more clearly and change your perception of stress by giving yourself the tools to deal with it effectively, or even to make it a precious ally.

COPING MECHANISMS: THE BASICS

WHAT IS STRESS?

To beat stress effectively, it is important to have an accurate understanding of it. While theorists on stress have given it more than one definition across the years, sometimes associating it with a trigger event and sometimes with the reaction incited in the person who is dealing with it, Lazarus is the first to perceive it as the relationship between these two things. Thus, today we speak of stress when an individual considers the demands of a situation he is faced with to be greater than his abilities, thus creating an imbalance between what is expected of him and what he thinks he is capable of. Stress is therefore no more part of the situation than it is of the individual that responds to it, it is rather in the interpretation that the individual has of it. That is why two different people will not necessarily react in the same way to the same event.

- Give new responsibilities to one person and they will joyfully welcome the news, seeing it as a mark of trust and the undoubtable sign of professional development. Give them to another on the other hand and you will see them crumble, terrified at the idea of not being up to the task.
- Made redundant due to restructuring, one person will force themselves to see their exit as a new challenge and an opportunity to take stock of their lives; the other will wrongly believe that they are fully responsible for their misfortunes, will lose all self-confidence and will have an

unbelievable struggle to pick themselves back up.

Moreover, these same people will not necessarily react in the same way to events throughout their career. Thus, an experienced employee will undoubtedly welcome new duties more calmly than they did at the start of their career. On the other hand, they could find it more difficult to deal with being fired than they did when they first set foot in the world of work, when no one was dependent on their income.

STRESSFUL SITUATIONS: A MATTER OF FRAMING

But if there are no fundamentally stressful situations, why do some events lead us to work ourselves up into a state while others seem to pass us by without affecting us? As stress develops in the relationship between the person and their environment, the answer to our question can necessarily be found somewhere between these two.

If we believe Lazarus and other supporters of his coping theory, we insert a series of filters between us and any situations we face, and these directly influence our perceptions of them. They are what does or does not trigger a stress reaction and, in that case, amplify or minimise its negative impact on our bodies, accentuating or reducing the feeling of discomfort that we feel towards the situation. These different filters, mediators of the relationship we have with our environment and the context in which we are developing, are as numerous as they are varied. While it is impossible to list all of them, some of the more poignant ones stand out from the list and are easy to round up.

Experience of the situation

Have we already faced this kind of event in the past? If so, did we manage to overcome the challenge without conflicts or do we still have bad memories of it?

If you are used to public speaking, you will certainly find it less difficult to give a tricky presentation than another who has never had the experience. In the same way, if you have already had strict deadlines to meet and you have done so, you will also feel less pressurised when a similar situation arises than if you are regularly reprimanded for not having managed to meet them.

Personality

Perfectionist and fussy individuals will be quicker to become subjects of stress than relaxed and casual people, in the same way as competitive workers will be more sensitive to the pressure of results than dabblers who do not find them important. There are some character traits that make an individual predisposed to stress and anxiety and others that shield individuals from it.

Beliefs and self-esteem

Maybe you have a tendency to blame destiny for the challenges you face, putting bad news and bad luck down to fate? Maybe you believe more in yourself and your ability to deal with any difficulties? Or maybe it's the opposite and you lack self-assurance and self-confidence, to the point of losing all control as soon as you are out of your comfort zone?

Your beliefs and your self-esteem inevitably condition the way you judge a situation. It is therefore obvious that you will feel the effects of stress less if you are convinced that you can deal with any kind of situation rather than if you have no faith in your own abilities.

Loved ones

Unconditional moral support from a loving family, the willingness of devoted friends to listen, the practical help of obliging colleagues and the recognition of a boss who values you (or employees who admire and respect you) will be great assets in your ability to deal with problems calmly. On the other hand, a divided family, toxic friendships, jealous colleagues and a boss who disregards you to the point of not even knowing your first name will all be facilitators of stress.

A healthy lifestyle

A healthy and varied diet, good sleep habits and regular physical activity make you feel good and you will automatically be in favourable conditions for facing daily problems.

Conscious mechanisms

Some people consciously fight against stress and anxiety through methods and mechanisms that are expressly used for this purpose. Thus, sport, yoga or relaxation sessions, regular breaks from working, having a drink in the bar on the corner to unwind after a challenging day and monthly sessions with a psychologist are all very effective ways of boosting your ability to manage anxiety.

FILTERS AND THEIR ROLE

These different filters, acting as intermediaries between us and our environment, determine and regulate our relationship to the world, but do not all carry out the same role.

- Evaluation: through criteria such as our personal experience and our confidence in our abilities, we evaluate the situation that presents itself to us and assess its potential danger based on our resources. Thus, does facing this event mean running a risk, taking our abilities into account? Should the situation we are dealing with be worrying to us? If so, to what extent?
- Coping: once this evaluation has been carried out, other filters such as conscious mechanisms and lifestyle come into play, becoming tools for coping, of which the aim is to reduce the effects of stress generated by the situation as much as possible, going as far as getting rid of any trace of them if possible.

COPING STRATEGIES

While there are many ways of fighting stress and reducing its effects, Lazarus and theorists of coping have managed, through their research, to classify these different methods and strategies into two distinct categories, expressing two completely opposite ways of dealing with and responding to situations that generate stress:

- Strategies centred on the problem (or confrontation strategies). Faced with a situation that is out of their control, supporters of confrontation strategies focus their attention on the problem and try to take control of it by facing it head-on, whether by gathering as much information as possible on the subject or by establishing a plan of action aimed at allowing them to regain control of the events. Coping mechanisms centred on the problem try to eliminate the problem at its source by directly confronting the causes of the stress.
- Strategies centred on emotion (or avoidance strategies). Users of avoidance strategies, on the other hand, tend to focus on themselves and their emotions, taking their focus off the problem to reduce its emotional impact as much as possible. Far from confronting the problematic situation itself, coping mechanisms centred on emotion rather endeavour to reduce its consequences on the individual.

Whichever coping methods and strategies you prefer, they will definitely correspond to one of these two categories.

In a situation that makes you anxious, you might be someone who prefers to attack the problem head-on. Nervous about speaking in public, you spend the weeks leading up to your speech reading a great deal of books on the subject and getting informed on the tips and tricks of the greatest orators.

Stressed at the thought of not finishing a job within the deadline, you embrace the challenge and spend countless hours on it, refusing to take a moment's break. Annoyed at a colleague or employee, you have a discussion with them to air your concerns.

On the other hand, you might be more inclined to look for relief elsewhere, preferring to think about anything other than the problem. Hurt by the incessant criticisms of your boss, you release the pressure by working up a sweat in the gym. Anxious a few minutes before a crucial presentation, you try to relax by thinking about something else or smoking one last cigarette. In a delicate position within your company, you abandon yourself to fate, convincing yourself that nothing happens by chance and that, whatever happens, there is a good reason for it.

Finally, it is also possible to combine several of these strategies, burning countless toxins and calories before going back in, with a calm and clear mind, and facing the problem.

EFFECTIVENESS AND LIMITATIONS OF THEORY

An adapted coping strategy

On a fundamental level, coping strategies centred on the problem are no more effective than the methods that are focused on emotion and vice versa, much like there is no miracle response which works in all circumstances. A strategy is effective if it achieves its aim, in this case to successfully reduce anxiety and get rid of the feelings of discomfort and imbalance felt in a given situation. Nonetheless, certain coping mechanisms are more or less helpful to implement depending on the type of situation you are facing.

- Thus, faced with an event that is beyond our control and that we cannot fight against, a 'passive' avoidance strategy will generally get better results. A worker who is being fired, for example, will accept the situation more easily by resigning himself to the inevitable rather than trying to fight in vain. As it is impossible to resolve the problem at its source, it is preferable to try to reduce its consequences as much as possible by adapting as much as we can.
- On the other hand, an 'active' strategy which is resolutely focused on the problem will, in most cases, be more effective in the event that it is possible to take control of the situation, requiring some effort. A young freelancer worried about launching their first small business will thus strongly reduce their anxiety by proactively getting informed on the risks of similar companies and by esta-blishing a plan of action aimed at guaranteeing success.

By simply following this basic rule of trying to choose the right strategy based on whether or not you can control the worrying event, it becomes possible to avoid a great deal of pitfalls found in the business world and to get rid of most of our bad habits, which harm our wellbeing and our productivity.

Bad habits that generate stress

When used well, the coping concept can help you to get rid of these annoying and counter-productive tendencies.

- Procrastination. It is tempting to put off annoying and time-consuming tasks, but putting off the moment when you have to deal with them will earn you nothing more than a little respite that you will have to pay off with interest. Files that pile up, delays to make up for, late nights working, etc.; so many problems and useless stress that you could save yourself from by avoiding letting things drag on. Remember: when it is possible to act in a situation, facing the problem frankly will generally be more effective than spending your time avoiding it.
- Perfectionism. Always bear in mind these two unalterable principles: it is impossible to please everyone; perfection does not exist. What is perfect to you is not necessarily perfect in your boss's eyes, and vice versa. Be demanding, of yourself and of others, but be careful not to have unmeasured expectations, in which case you risk starting to feel frustrated. The impact that you have on what other people think will always be limited. If you are doing your best and that is not enough, look for a way to reduce the consequences of the situation on your state of mind by adopting an avoidance strategy (exercising, relaxing, relativising, etc.) rather than spending your time looking for others' approval.
- The need to control everything. Some situations are beyond your control and you can do nothing about them. Fierce competition due to the markets' opening, being made redundant for an economic reason, a resolutely

jealous colleague, a fundamentally unpleasant head of department, etc. It would be pointless to try to tackle the problem at its source in these circumstances, it is better to focus on your emotions.

- The fear of saying 'no'. Your days are not extendable: if you are already overwhelmed with work, do not add even more to your workload for fear of seeming like a slacker, incapable or an unfriendly colleague. If someone is trying to assign you a task which is not in your remit, be firm and tell the other person this. If you are underqualified or rushed for time, you will feel that you are not up to the task and this may even start to fuel resentment towards whoever put you in this uncomfortable situation as well as towards yourself for not having managed to say 'no'. As the decision is up to you, do not look for a solution by fleeing: face the problem head-on by eliminating the potential stress at its source.
- Forgetting about interpersonal relationships. Whatever your position within the company, a harmful work atmosphere and conflictual professional relationships will undoubtedly lead to a collective loss of motivation and a general reduction in productivity. Conversely, good cohesion between colleagues and good relationships between bosses and employees will guarantee all workers a better resistance to sources of stress inherent to the world of business. If you feel that the atmosphere is not great, start a discussion to lay everything out and restart from a healthy starting point.
- The fear of asking for help. Sometimes the storm is particularly difficult to ride out, and nothing is forcing you to deal with them alone. There is no shame in asking for

support from loved ones, colleagues, or even professionals who might help you to overcome these challenges. It is never helpful to keep things to yourself and deal with your doubts alone, and the simple act of opening up to someone will already feel like a weight off your shoulders. Whether you have tried a confronting strategy unsuccessfully, leaving you helpless, or have sought refuge in an avoidance strategy with the aim of protecting yourself, it is time to change tactic. Going to see someone you trust means working both on the emotional impact of the situation and on the origins of the problem.

- Non-stop work. While it is not good to succumb to procrastination, it is also not good to never give yourself time to relax. Take time for yourself, as it is necessary to unwind regularly to recharge and avoid overworking. Exercise, read, go out. In short, change what you are thinking about.
- Addictions. Alcohol, nicotine, caffeine, anti-anxiety drugs, etc. are all substances that can easily lead to an addiction if we are not careful. In small doses, they can certainly help you to relax, but they can quickly become counter-productive and cause enormous damage. Bear in mind that moderation is necessary in everything. While avoidance strategies are not inherently bad, fleeing the situation has never resolved anything.

When stress becomes inevitable

While the theory of coping is particularly effective for analysing and therefore better managing stressful situations and moments of psychological tension, it would obviously be presumptuous and unrealistic to imagine that it is possible to put a definitive end to stress at work through its intervention.

As we have seen, the way we interpret the events we are faced with as well as our resistance to stress depend on many different criter a and do not solely rely on the different strategies we implement to deal with them. While it is completely possible to be able to choose in your mind and conscience a type of response to provide in a given situation based on its characteristics, the variables are what makes it difficult – or in scme cases impossible – to influence. Thus, our personalities, through the character traits that constitute our identity, make us more or less predisposed to stress, making us more or less sensitive to situations that are likely to cause it, without our being able to do anything. In the same way, we cannot feign experience: it is difficult to react like a seasoned professional to a situation we have never experienced, whatever efforts we make to deal with it.

It is important not to lose sight of the fact that coping theory, while it gives us the tools to learn how to master the effects of stress and lessen its problems, does not permanently rid us of the problem, as much as it could also turn out to be very useful in certain circumstances.

STRESS: AN ALLY

In fact, while it is obvious that in too large an amount, stress can have disastrous consequences on our wellbeing and our health, inflicting physical harm (cardiac problems, high blood pressure, stomach ulcers, skin problems, significant weight loss or gain, etc.) and psychological harm (mental fatigue, irritability, tendencies for depression and isolation, etc.), the right dose of stress can be beneficial and improve our performance at work, as long as we know how to take advantage of it.

Thus, the increase of adrenaline in the bloodstream and the acceleration of the heartbeat that result from it can briefly improve our physical and intellectual abilities, giving our bodies welcome extra energy and our brains increased agility, making us temporarily more effective. In the same way, stress and its various manifestations can act as excellent signals of danger, advance indications that something serious and harmful is lurking in the shadows. Constantly tense muscles, persistent migraines, shooting pain, increasingly irritable behaviour, hypersensitivity and higher consumption of alcohol, coffee or even chocolate are all signs you ought to look out for if you want to avoid the unfortunately famous burnout syndrome.

While the devastating effects of severe stress no longer need to be proven and it is important to equip yourself to deal with it adequately, it is also essential not to forget that stress can also be useful, productive and encouraging, often proving itself indispensable to succeeding in the most demanding challenges. Not all stress is bad, you just need to learn to manage it.

TOP TIPS

- Work on your self-esteem. You have not been recruited by accident but because someone believed that you have the necessary abilities to meet the demands of your role. So why should you doubt this? Trust in your ability to adapt to new situations, and use your past experiences to do this. Wasn't there a first time for all of the tasks that you can now do effortlessly and almost without thinking about it?

- In the same way, learn to put things into perspective. Never forget that what used to make you nervous probably no longer troubles you now. There is no reason why what you are currently worried about will not meet the same fate. It is therefore useless to make a mountain out of a molehill: put things into perspective and relativise.

- Accept your mistakes. No one is perfect, and your colleagues and superiors also make them from time to time. Your work alone is not what defines you, and your life does not begin when you walk through your office's doors. You are much more than that, so why should fleeting professional difficulties necessarily mean that you are worth nothing? Simply take responsibility and look for a solution.

- Look after yourself. Having a healthy, balanced diet, good sleep patterns and doing regular exercise will not definitely protect you from stress, but it will allow you to deal with the issues of office life in the best possible conditions. On the other hand, regularly resorting to stimulants such as caffeine, tobacco and alcohol will only make you fragile, making you more susceptible to potentially stressful stimuli. Build yourself a fortress, not a tomb.

- Take time for yourself and learn how to disconnect. Your professional life is important, there is no doubt about that, but it should not overtake your personal life at any point. While it is sometimes acceptable to let the office follow you home, especially if you are faced with some fleeting difficulties or when an important presentation is on the horizon, it shouldn't worry you constantly. Have a life outside of work. Cleanse your mind of the worries you have at work by regularly doing an activity that relaxes you. Going for walks, going to the gym, starting yoga, a cooking course, painting, pottery, etc. The possibilities are varied and numerous.

- Find a person you trust to talk to. Whether it is a relative, a friend, a colleague or a specialist, it is essential to be able to count on being listened to attentively by someone to whom you can freely entrust your doubts and worries. With the benefit of distance that you do not necessarily have from the situation, this person you trust will help you to relativise your problems, and will maybe even be able to give you some things to think about that you hadn't thought of yourself. Additionally, the simple act of putting your problems into words and expressing them aloud will lift a weight off your shoulders and do you a world of good. Burying your worries and keeping them to yourself is not the solution, as building up increasing tension can, in the long term, only lead to implosion (depression, burnout, etc.) or explosion (being quick to anger, uncontrolled and irrational aggression, etc.).

FAQS

WHERE DO I START IN IMPLEMENTING A PERSONAL COPING STRATEGY?

To implement an effective personal coping strategy, the important thing above all is to ask the right questions:

- What factors influence my relationship to the world around me and the perception I have of my environment and the events that happen in my life? Education, age, gender, self-esteem, lifestyle, social circle? To what extent does the stress I am feeling stem from them, and what can I change about them?
- Which mechanisms have I consciously implemented to fight stress and its effects? To what extent and in which circumstances are these effective? Could I make use of others? If so, which ones?
- Am I on a level playing field with the situation that is causing me stress, in that I can deal with it? Or would I be better off trying to reduce its consequences on my wellbeing and productivity through different means?

WHAT IS THE BEST WAY OF OVERCOMING STRESS?

Unfortunately, there is no miracle method that allows us to rid ourselves of stress once and for all, just as there are no coping strategies that are more effective than others, independent of the context and characteristics of the stressful event. All coping methods are potentially effective, as long as they are used appropriately.

Thus, in the event that a situation is beyond our control, such as being fired for economic reasons, you are advised to try to limit its consequences through an avoidance strategy centred on emotion. Calming yourself through relaxation or physical exercise, for example, is therefore preferred.

When it is possible to act directly to change the problematic situation, on the other hand, it is generally more profitable to try to resolve the problem at its source, directly addressing the causes. In a harmful work environment, for example, a discussion to expose the causes of the general bad atmosphere should be had, rather than trying to reduce the negative impact of the situation.

HOW DO I FIGURE OUT THE BEST COPING STYLE FOR ME?

Simply reflect on your own habits. How do you generally react in stressful situations? Are you someone who puts off facing the problem for as long as possible, or are you someone who wants to be in control of everything to reassure yourself? Are you used to having a drink after work to forget the personal problems you have with your colleagues or do you prefer to use your energy on reflecting on the best way to sort things out with them?

It is, however, perfectly possible that you do not have a preferred style per se. Thus, you might use problem-focused strategies in some circumstances, whilst opting for emotion-focused strategies in others, based on your past experiences.

WHAT HARMFUL HABITS SHOULD I AVOID?

Avoidance strategies are not harmful, far from it: it is very important to learn how to manage the effects of anxiety on our bodies and minds. But it is even more essential not to come up with escape strategies.

One drink to relax after a stressful day or a cigarette to calm your nerves before an important meeting are not inherently bad habits, but it is important with similar substances to make sure you do not succumb to excess, which can lead to addiction. This would only increase your stress while causing irreversible damage to your physical and psychological health. Dealing with your sources of stress at one moment or another is still generally indispensable.

IS IT POSSIBLE TO LIVE A STRESS-FREE LIFE THANKS TO COPING MECHANISMS?

A completely stress-free life is impossible, with or without coping mechanisms. This technique gives us the means to respond effectively, helps us to reduce the negative impacts on our bodies and sometimes even allows us to get rid of the causes, but it will never manage to free us from it completely, as independent variables such as our personality and our experience also have an impact on our ability to resist stress.

Such freedom from stress would in any case not be desirable, as stress can turn out to be useful, notably when it

brings us the extra energy necessary for accomplishing certain tasks, or as a way of drawing our attention to potential,
more serious problems lurking in the shadows (depression,
burnout, etc.).

OVER TO YOU

There is no magic method that applies to all situations and works every time. Managing stress is not always easy, nor even doable. As we have seen, however, it is often possible to protect ourselves from it and to have a calmer view of the situations we cannot escape from. To do this, you simply need to head in the right direction with a good plan of action. And that plan of action is up to you to establish!

Rest assured, there is nothing too complicated about this. Simply use what you have just learned. By applying a frame of reference to each situation, with the aim of bringing the reasons for this perception to light, the different possibilities for recommended responses will emerge automatically.

Plan of action

Stressful situation	Reasons for stress	Problem-focused coping strategy	Emotion-focused coping strategy
First presentation in front of my supervisor	• Lack of experience	• Ask for advice from someone with more experience • Get informed • Train myself	• Remember the other times I was new to a task that went well
Producing a long and complex document	• Fear of being judged for my work by my supervisor, as I am a perfectionist	• Give myself a time limit for completing this task and stick to it	• Relativize
Reorganisation within the company	• A situation that is completely out of my control	• Ask for an evaluation from my supervisor and work on what I need to • Look for another job as soon as possible	• Exercise • Talk about it to a loved one

Remember that everyone is different and that, while there are some universal truths, what works for you is not necessarily what works for the people around you and vice versa. Also, feel free to take note of the strategies that turned out to be particularly effective at dealing with what was worrying you and in which circumstances, and which methods did not have the hoped-for effects. You alone can precisely determine the most suitable plan of action.

FURTHER READING

BIBLIOGRAPHY

- Bruchon-Schweitzer, M. (2001) Le coping et les stratégies d'ajustement face au stress. *Recherche en soins infirmiers*. Issue 67. Toulouse: A.R.S.I. pp. 68-83.
- Brun, J.-P. and Martel, J. (2003) *La santé psychologique au travail. De la définition du problème aux solutions.* Geneva: Chaire en gestion de la santé et de la sécurité du travail dans les organisations de l'Université Laval.
- Bureau International du Travail. (1993) Le stress dans le monde du travai.. *Le travail dans le monde*. Geneva: Bureau International du Travail.
- Durand Uberti, M.-L. (No date) Travail : la bonne méthode pour gérer son stress. *Psychologies.com*. [Online]. [Accessed 2 November 2014]. Available from: <http://www.psychologies.com/Travail/Souffrance-au-travail/Stress-au-travail/Articles-et-Dossiers/Travail-la-bonne-methode-pour-gerer-son-stress>
- Fontana, D. (1990) *Gérer le stress*. Brussels: Mardaga.
- Hazanov-Boskovitz, O. (2003) *Étude du coping des adolescents dans un contexte expérimental*. [PhD thesis]. Geneva: Université de Genève.
- Nogues-Ledru, M.-P. (No date) 10 pistes pour retrouver confiance en soi au travail. *L'express.fr*. [Online]. [Accessed 2 November 2014]. Available from: <http://www.lexpress.fr/emploi/gestion-carriere/10-pistes-pour-retrouver-confiance-en-soi-au-travail_1320649.html>
- Paulhan, I. (1992) Le concept de coping. *L'Année Psychologique*. Issue 92. Paris: NecPlus. pp. 545-557.

- Piquemal-Vieu, L. (2001) Le coping une ressource à identifier dans le soin infirmier. *Recherche en soins infirmiers*. Issue 67. Toulouse: A.RS.I. pp. 84-97.

ADDITIONAL SOURCES

- Boyes, A. (2015) *The Anxiety Toolkit*. New York: TarcherPerigee.
- Rao, S. (2010) *Happiness at Work*. New York: McGraw-Hill Education.
- Dalai Lama and Cutler, H. C. (2004) *The Art of Happiness at Work*. New York: Riverhead.

www.50minutes.com

Ebook EAN: 9782806289162

Paperback EAN: 9782806289179

Legal Deposit: D/2016/12603/741

Cover: © Primento

Digital conception by Primento, the digital partner of publishers.